# HOROSCOPE OF THE MOON

### Zofia Ilinska

TABB HOUSE

First published 1992
Tabb House, 7 Church Street, Padstow, Cornwall, PL28 8BG

A catalogue record for this book is available from the British Library

Printed by Quintrells Colour Printers Ltd, Wadebridge
and bound by T. J. Press Ltd, Padstow

'Aikichi Kuboyama' has appeared in *London Magazine*; *The Guinness Book of Poetry, 1956/7*; *Anthology of Modern Verse, 1940-1960*; *Anthology of English Poetry, 1945-1960*; *New Poems — a PEN Anthology*; *German Anthology Lion and Unicorn*; *Poems from Hospital* (Howard Sergeant); *Reach Out — School List Book Three* (1968); The BBC Third Programme; South African Broadcasting Corporation. It has been translated into Polish, German and Indonesian.

'The Poet reads the Horoscope of the Moon'; *London Magazine; Guinness Book of Poetry, 1957/58;* BBC Third Programme.

'An Old Woman' — *London Magazine; New Poems 1960 — a PEN Anthology.*

'The Garment' — *Outposts, 1978.*

'The Refugee' — *London Magazine; New Poems 1963 — a PEN Anthology.* BBC Third Programme.

'Landscape with a Curlew' — *London Magazine.*

'Homo Neanderthal' — Stroud Festival 1967.

'Ruan Lanihorne' — *The Cornish Review,* 1970.

'Silence' — *London Magazine.*

'The Tanker and Her Tugs' — *The Cornish Review,* 1969.

'Perpetually I Mourn You' — *The Cornish Review,* 1973.

'The Room' — *New Poetry 4.* 1978; An Arts Council Anthology.

'Premonition' — *The Human World.*

'Aikichi Kuboyama', 'The Poet reads the Horoscope of the Moon', 'The Old Woman', 'The Refugee', 'Homo Neanderthal' and 'Cantata for Apple Voices' have appeared in '*Wiadomosci* London', translated by Beata Obertynska into Polish.

'When I return to Poland' is to be published by *Outposts*.

To the editors of these magazines and radio programmes the author and publisher would like to make due acknowledgment.

# FOREWORD

In the act of writing, Zofia Ilinska proclaims her purpose, and that of her art. The function of the poet is to be a poet, if only for herself. Her published work, in Polish and in English, has been for the most part, of a public character; but this new collection includes a large group of poems which were written, I suspect, with little expectation of being heard: poems 'written for the drawer'. Not that these works are difficult, abstruse or delphic. They are nothing of the kind; they are simply intensely private. But the nature of Ilinska's private vision encompasses the whole of humanity. She takes the reader by the arm, and 'are you not poets also?' she seems to say, 'and are not these joys and tragedies also yours?' In the blackest of times she searches for meaning in the innocences of the world that lies within the grasp of her own senses. Like a bee, she probes the 'dark tender-throated nectary . . . so that not a scent be lost, not a pollen of that life'. In that world she finds that the meaning of life is to live and to search and to live again. The practice of a private art thus becomes a public event. Her voice, now dark, now humorous, now ironic, sometimes elusive, usually direct, is always human, always sane.

Tim Retallack, 1992

# CONTENTS

Page

Foreword
TROUBLE IN THE WORLD

Trouble in the World                                          1
The Moan of Cassandra                                        2
Contradictions                                               4
The Child looks at the Moon                                  5
The Scarecrow                                                6
Timor Mortis                                                 7
The Poet reads the Horoscope of the Moon                     8
The Skyscraper                                               9
The Century drifts into Afternoon                           13
Aikichi Kuboyama                                            15


CORNISH POEMS                                               17

Summer Happiness                                            19
Walks, Meditations                                          20
For the Season of Strawberries                              21
Ruan Lanihorne                                              22
The Rook                                                    24
The Poet envies the Oak                                     26
Saint Just in Roseland                                      27
The Sparrow                                                 28
The Moon Rolls Out                                          29
The Heron                                                   30
Bird's Prayer                                               31
Cantata for Apple Voices                                    32


THE ACCIDENT                                                37

I have taken Vows says the Moon                             39
Babybirds, Kittens                                          46

My Wishes for Him                              47
A Tonic Bomb says the Child                    48
Thoughts on Education                          49
Mother, Mother, Which is Better?               51
Premonition                                    52
Car Split in Three as it Hit Lorry             53
The Wild Night Horses Kill                     54
Silence                                        55
Have You Encountered Anyone Who Knows?         56
Remembering                                    57
If You Wish to be Immortal                     58
The Room                                       60
The Ever Mysterious Victim                     61
Natasha Says                                   62
Little Thoughts                                63
A Prayer                                       64
What are these Birds for?                      65

## LOVE POEMS AND OTHER POEMS                  67

Greece in Haikus                               69
The Refugee                                    72
The Tramp                                      74
An Old Woman                                   75
Homo Neanderthal                               76
I'd Love You Better                            77
Watched by a Robin                             78
Today as Always                                79
Landscape with a Curlew                        80
The Garment                                    81
Concerning Love                                82
When I Return to Poland                        87

# Trouble in the World

# TROUBLE IN THE WORLD

When all is well I do not write.
Why? It is not clear.
Perhaps in case my shoddy word
should blur the atmosphere.

Perhaps because my ALL IS WELL
in silence is complete.
Idle and blissful while it lasts
I bask at ALL WELL's feet

like the good oyster when he has
no need to roll his pearl.
I need my strong impediment:
trouble in the world.

# THE MOAN OF CASSANDRA

Ladies and gentlemen, long haired, short haired,
also the hairless, having made the effort
to attend this feast of the arts, spare me five minutes
of undivided attention: am I not the curious
phenomenon of the Age, the NUCLEAR POET,
evolving Homo Sapiens post coitum triste,
balanced at conscious point
of skyscraper Race?

Schizophrenic, uncertified, indestructible as the rabbit,
threatened by virus, threatened by pollution,
threatened by unknown, morbid mutations of matter,
shy of machine-life, nervous of radiation
I pick my symbols from molecules, protons
to record the dread of the Age, its blindfold look,
the electronic buzz, the circuit of death.

> The tiger perishes
> The wild tiger perishes
> The blue whale perishes
> The giant panda
> The unborn child perishes
> The mottled thrush.

I am the poet who sings
Mostly to myself.
My chanting skirmishes round dark enigmas
I hold more lives than the cat
I clutch, I cling
To my allotted quota of affection and pain
Scribbling, recording
Praising common goodness,
Patiently grunting at mediocrity.

Art is aristocratic, poule de luxe
Ladies and gentlemen, put by your steaks,
Revive the rituals, participate.
The air is murderous. My language is mournful.

# CONTRADICTIONS

"Granted through prayer a glimpse beyond that Curtain
I found some of the prospects exquisite.
You see, one ought to cultivate a certain
Bravado to explore the infinite."

And there among the rudiments of death
And shades of hurting propped against the pillows
A sudden kitten-gesture caught my breath
As if the wind played in the pussy willows.

I thought you childlike, beautiful and rash
And almost could accuse you of a pose;
As if it were preposterous to disclose
Beneath the withering dismay of flesh
The crimson meditations of the rose.

# THE CHILD LOOKS AT THE MOON

"In your window hangs one moon.
Another moon in mine.
I shall eat them with a silver spoon
And then they will cease to shine."

"O do not touch them" — cried the child,
"For though they gleam and glitter,
They are monster apples: silver-hard
And old and golden-bitter."

# THE SCARECROW

I wish there was no thought in me.
This head of thought exhausteth me,
this head of trouble, head of thought . . .
Could I but wear a scarecrow's coat
and left alone, without a care
flap at the passing world and stare
at leaf and bird and pigeon wing,
or nothing, no thing, not a thing . . .
I wish there was no thought in me.
This head of thought exhausteth me.

Neighboured by speechless trees, alone,
straw upon straw, not flesh and bone,
a leg of wood in thoughtless grass,
I'd watch the summers rise and pass,
I — scarecrow of the garden site —
tormented by no itch to write,
no angst, no need to chase for words,
just stick where stuck and flap at birds
with merry sleeves of rag and straw.
No need to ask — no urge to know,
no love, no longing, no desire,
not set on fire, not setting fire,
not fearing this, not hoping that . . .
Beneath my draughty borrowed hat,
lump-of-coal eyes and carrot nose
I would make faces at the crows
causing the passers-by to gaze
at the old scarecrow's silly face.
In time I would just fall apart
without a pang of head or heart
and not a pair of eyes would weep
for Scarecrow on the rubbish heap.
Alone some pilgrim-bird may know
his nest was pleated in my straw.
I wish there was no thought in me.
This head of thought exhausteth me.

# TIMOR MORTIS

There was delirium inside my head,
There was a ticking in the thermostat,
There was a crazy desiccated beat
Circled eleven times about the bed,
There was a ticking in the thermostat,
When quietly my eldest frock-coat said
To all the others: "I am sure of that;
I am the one in which he will lie dead."

I heard wool-whispers, smackings of the lips
Along the buttons, button-holes and zips.
They strained on hangers, they were all on edge
Curious of the old frock-coat's privilege
Who blurted out: "When Soul its Body leaves,
Timor Mortis hisses down the sleeves."

# THE POET READS THE HOROSCOPE OF THE MOON

*It seems that poetry in all ages is the*
*attempt to find new images for the moon*

Through moonlit lattices I watch you go
Half-beast, half-glow-worm in your dome of glass
Swaying a little upon windy corners;
Your shades of crocus, dandelion, dough,
Pale saffron yellow, ale, cream, honey, straw;
Solitudes planted all along your path;
Your crazy golden braying: "yo-ho-ho".
You make me think of Apuleius' Ass.

Luminous Images: moon-this, moon-that:
Chiselled, chill, crooked alabaster tusk;
Moon of the setting sun, the rising bat;
Small moon of dawn and little moon of dusk;
Moon wrapped in mist and moon wrapped in mildew;
Wild garlic moon, mint-moon and moon of musk;
Bent diamond trinket tarnished with the dew
Step down — I would weep for you —
Down, down — I would weep, weep for you,
Because your horoscopes foretell great loss:
Ah, they desert you all — shape, texture, tone
Of owlsoft night, mosaic of leaf and moss,
The elegiac quality of stone,
Nightingale singing: "Poor, poor Itylus . . ."

This is no age for dreams: Desert your throne,
Roll down the centuries your heavy crown.
Your power, your calm, your interstellar drone,
The worn-out splendour of your borrowed gown
Are glories of the past. The world is sick
And you have reached the Phase of Discontent

To wax and wane upon concrete and brick,
Inscrutable on mortar and cement,
With terror-cables for your lack of trees,
Neon-lights poking craters in your sockets,
Pneumatic drills to drain your arid seas:

A whitewashed platform waiting for the rockets.

# THE SKYSCRAPER

*Like the nude, the building represents a balance
between an ideal scheme and functional necessities.*

I do not know much about architecture
but let me confess
that I consider this arrangement of straight solid
massive brutal unbroken malevolent
layers of flatness upon flatness
beautiful.

Granite flatness upon granite flatness
in slabs of geometrical glass concrete and plastic
beautiful.

Look, how it rises to meet dawn, the Colossus,
awkward and stooping in the face of the rising sun
and at dusk when sunset arranges
the harmonies of fourteen layers
into something like pink tenderness,
its high nocturnal aspect lit up and majestic,
great liner riding the breakers
into the teeth of machine-age midnight,
beautiful.

And O let us smile at the minute lace curtain let loose
on the thirteenth floor flapping at the wind,
absurd incongruous flighty
wayward irreverent.

## II

Note how the latent warmth of human flesh
seeps into stone where flesh has made its lair.
Note how the elevator fills the stair
case as the stone the avocado pear.

Note how typewriter — cooker — frigidaire
witness to squareness. Note: the Age is square.
Reflect: faith lifted spires into the air.
Doubt builds skyscrapers. Doubt, no doubt, is square.

Do you understand why the Circle has been discarded, why
the curve and hollow rejected, why
baroque dismissed?
Who said the behind is a baroque form? Why
Gothic and the sloping alphabets of mystery?
The white 'face of the Infanta peering down
from the burning Estoril'.
Gargoyles observing slaughter have become
ghosts of a past that inhabited different houses.
I know of no reason for the abdication of the Circle.
I only know that in the alphabets of concrete
I read of tremendous denials,
being no longer able to decipher the syllables of
exultation rapturous freedom,
memory of rocks and caves and kneeling forms,
women and grapes and round things
out of the warm wild earth.

This is an abstract age.

### III

The pull of space, you have said,
economics of structure,
pressures of scientific revolution,
in no way a cult of the ugly,
for you must notice how
at the groin of intersection,
austerely,
wall and buttress converge in harmony,
sheltering incomprehensible energy
like a child holding a stone.

We cannot comprehend the Age.
It is not yet ended.
Sons build not as fathers built
in styles you may call brutal
but which are necessary styles,
to protect us from evils
we may not as yet be aware of.
Watch the rise of this square construction,
for is it not growing into your grandchild's fortress against
unpredictable epidemics of traffic,
explosions of noise,
infections of lorries revving uphill,
tiny whines of Polos and baby Austins
weaned from second into bottom gear
yelling in terrible exhaustion of repressed speed
killing another man's silence.
And not traffic. Not traffic only.
Square one of the solid walls protect us
from miasmas of noise that may crack our skulls.

And let us wonder, let us wonder if ever
in what leap century, under which burnt out satellite,
which new born crater, owing to what Act of God,
what unaccountable vibration, what bang in the scheme
of eternal cogitations,
will the snail and termite review
the laws and rhythms of their baroque and gothic?

# THE CENTURY DRIFTS INTO AFTERNOON

*We have only just cast off the last moorings*
*which held us to the Neolithic Age.*

The room is full of poets. As I stand
gathering the whispers of the Sacred Grove
one limp and lonely like a trumpet fish
and as if worn searching a faultless love
touches my hand.
We talk of atoms — magazines — the moon —
he cruises nearer the fire spilling ash —
    the century drifts into afternoon . . .

I feel so wide awake — he says — I'd leap
into the sun and through our modern tools
follow the plunge of planets underneath,
the agitation of the molecules
watch the earth sweep
past with her cargo of red cell and bone.
Who is it called her 'old bitch gone in the teeth'?
    the century drifts into afternoon . . .

How smooth she runs, the sun's brown flying kite,
like a baked apple, wrinkled and magenta
hoarding primeval footprints in the snow,
chasing in orbits, giving cries of light
round boiling centres!
Amazing mass of matter on the run,
will she lose her electrons spinning so?
    the century drifts into afternoon . . .

In this half white half yellow midday glare
all that I notice perplexes the eye:
the cabled seas, the prowling submarine,
the unknown object buzzing in the sky,
the electric air . . .

the noonday devil pokes about the stone
plans cruelty — power — levity — coldness — sin —
    the century drifts into afternoon . . .

and what a trepidation at the lights!
wheel presses hand, brake importunes the foot,
brain changes gears, vibrates with the machine
secreting fumes, concern with its own output
fear, rocket sites . . .
Markets are being flooded with misfortune
refugees — famine — pepper — penicillin —
    the century drifts into afternoon . . .

And here goes man clutching his pain and purse
strapped to his chariot — anxious — tense — alone —
suddenly notices his gear is gone
into reverse.
The cosmic trappings are rushed back to town,
his botched powers fester like a fall from grace
    the century drifts into afternoon . . .

I see him as a mixer of cement
who prunes skyscrapers, saddles a waterfall
dissects a wriggling incongruity,
looks for a god to decorate his wall
and he ferments
in juice of steak — speed — sterling — terylene —
fearing — I think — discomfort terribly.
    the century drifts into afternoon . . .

So he reverses under ticking clocks
into the arched penumbras of the square.
The lily of his field gives up the ghost,
his eagle hatches missiles of the air
on thousand rocks.
O grant him space inside the Parking Zone
O grant him time inside the Parking Zone
    the century drifts into afternoon . . .

# AIKICHI KUBOYAMA

*The world's first-known hydrogen bomb
victim died yesterday in a Tokyo hospital after
an illness of six months; Aikichi Kuboyama, a
fisherman, on the boat* Lucky Dragon.
*Western Morning News.* Sept. 24th 1954

Come closer. Watch the newly-born disease.
I am Aikichi Kuboyama, stranger.
Aikichi Kuboyama, Japanese:
Small boat. Strong fish. Yellow sea. Very danger.
Nose to the wind. Seasalt. Seasharp. Seaspeck
Of mushroom cloud higher than Fuji. Heat.
I — fingers in the fishnets upon deck,
I — sick and yellow underneath the sheet,
Life squeezed into the smallness of a pill
Tasting of milk as when it first began,
Stillness for one that never would keep still,
Dream for a very dreaming kind of man
That worked for not too long and took to bed
But in his time fished hard in stream and sea
And loved the fall of blossom on the head,
And blessed o-cha, the aromatic tea,
And owned too much in sea, too little in soil:
Green mulberry, brown worm, kimono blue
And lived on octopus thick-sliced and boiled
Octopus eyes that gaze inside of you.

Night. Torches. Cormorants in pitch-pine heat.
Nagara river dances in the dusk
Slow softly swaying on tabi-clad feet.
Go, feed the holy horse on holy rusk.
Go, find the cormorants. O, find the place
Between the whirlpools. Find and tell me how
Downstream past Gifu (wind upon the face)
In water-lapping dactyls water splashes
Against the heart, against the tar-stained bow.
Aikichi Kuboyama dies of ashes.

# Cornish Poems

# SUMMER HAPPINESS

Mother, cook, driver, gardener, beachcomber
Driving down country lanes with flocks of young;
Surfing boards, picnic-baskets, ice-cream, song
I have not read a poem all the summer
Or even nibbled at a line of verse,
Yet must admit that in this busy mood
I fit so well into the universe
As if I'd never heard of solitude
Or known that special turmoil of the mind,
Creative thought. Partly-fulfilled I find
A simpler, easier, lazier happiness
In daily jobs repeated till the lids
Droop down with tiredness: lengthening a dress
Or stewing apples for a crowd of kids.

# WALKS, MEDITATIONS . . .

My walks are my meditations. While the dog
Sniffs around gathering secret messages,
Pauses to lift the energetic leg
Or leaps after a bird that vanishes,
I get on with my own kind of sniffing
Along the footpath which skirts the river,
Across the field, my patch of emotion,
Contained by the high gate and the low gate
To be opened or climbed over . . .
Sheep graze on the hill and thought grazes
Round horizons which please most and trouble most,
In pursuit of its own vanishing shapes, now rising
To a bird's eye view of life: satisfying.
Today sea and sky philosophise about time and space.
Today the heron preaches austerity.
Daisies add fresh footnotes to Plato.
Coupling wood-pigeons illuminate
Love between the sexes,
While divinely wet grass boasts and babbles
"I am soaked with happiness".
I lift the usual stone to find swarming beneath
A heap of tiny conclusions:
But which is the life most worth living?
The thought most worth recording?
Does it matter? As long as you hold
This acre of space and freedom
To stretch your stiffness in and breathe the wind,
Muttering to yourself: I am alive,
A warm thought inside your coat-pocket;
While the wings of God beat the air;
While gorse exudes its smell of coconut.

# FOR THE SEASON OF STRAWBERRIES

Lift a strawberry under a chin
Lay her sideways on layers of straw:
Without knocking the sun will come in
Through the circular strawberry door.

Venus, Venus asleep in the hush
Of a garden that never occurred,
You will find your seducer, the thrush,
The impeccable taste of the bird!

# RUAN LANIHORNE

Late December, early snow
Round the blunt and sleepy thorn.
Lady, lady will you go
With a twig of mistletoe
To meet your love at Lanihorne?

Every kingfisher you know,
Every quail was bred and born
In the rushes high and low
With minnows in the undertow
In Ruan Ruan Lanihorne.

Lady, lady, when you go
To Lanihorne, to Lanihorne
Thinking yes and thinking no,
Behold emerging from the snow
A little golden Unicorn.

You may see him dance and skip
On the high heraldic foot
While the willows sway and dip
Their swaying, weeping willow-tip
To sounds of the magic flute.

Gently stroke his pointed horn,
Gaze into his jewelled eyes
Ancient, wicked, gay, forlorn.
Give him whiffs of peppercorn
To sniff at till he cries.

And when he's still and out of breath
From dancing, tears and peppercorn
Ask him more and ask him less

Ask about love, life and death
In Ruan Ruan Lanihorne.

And he will answer yes and no
Nodding with his haunted horn.
Lady, lady will you go
With a twig of mistletoe
To meet your love at Lanihorne?

# THE ROOK

Already under the hill the sun beats
Like a soft drum. Already the first birdvoice
Stirs in the hedgerow. The rook wakes, yawns, stretches
Each stiff still sleepy muscle, gargles his throat
With the dawn, pulls on his black underwear,
His rugged plusfours, adjusts his collar
Loosely, for the air is warm. Chestnut buds
Have burst overnight; gorse hits him with yellow;
For a while he observes twin shoots of grass
Terribly buffeted by a blackbird,
Shakes with shock at their tiny uprootings.
Re-enters the room summoned by her who has shared
How many of their Aprils? Re-enters the room:
"Completely incomplete without you, my dark
Rook-woman. Let us go on building and
Rebuilding this house we together built."
He caresses her still appetising shoulder,
Abandons her to egg-absorption; not before
Dwelling in some detail upon the wild wind's
Last casualty;
Prospects of sons and neighbours; daughters
Given in marriage; timber obtained
For the marriage chamber. Registering the need
Of minor repairs in the doghair flooring,
He now acknowledges hunger, rejoicing,
For in the beech groves canteens are flung open,
While grub-traffic grows intense in the corridors
Of the shrubbery. Turning in his head
The agenda for the morning's first meeting,
He hurries off inhaling the world
With a guttural Caw-Caw —
Inflections of contented energy.
From the house below the poet watches
The beaky pilgrim of the branches

24

In his penniless kingdom half envying
The vitality of perennial breeding;
Comparing the antiquity of their races;
The security of their nests;
The steadfastness of their loves;
The eloquence of their comment upon
The business of living.

# THE POET ENVIES THE OAK

Autumnal forest. Pensive the path leads
through solitudes of juniper and fern.
Scattered upon the path in coral burn
mountain ash berries, broken necklace beads.
A violence of the wind throws into grass
a hundred acorns, loses them in heather
blowing into my head a sense of loss,
grief at the onset of my own October weather,
the little accomplished and the time it took.
Months, years, decades . . . I contemplate the oak,
his gift of time, the effortless and mild
gestures of spreading, the fat breeding look,
the acorn-poem and the acorn-child . . .
Delivered into grass. I am jealous of the oak.

# SAINT JUST IN ROSELAND

*Ecclesia Sancti Justi-de-Lansioch-in-Rose*

This is the place where the dead are moored
to everlasting buoys beside the boats.
The Creek is everywhere. The Church floats
like a seabird whose neck is the tower.
Flight of the heron to Turnaware.
     Bird country, boat country . . .

This is the place where the boats are moored
beside the churchyard, in green canvas dressed.
The dead sleep feet pointing East.
The seagull cries, voice wet and windy.
Growth — vegetation — stillness — beauty —
     Sea country, water country . . .

The Church is the Ark. I am Noah.
Here, I would save the seabirds first. The Hill
leans back, dark green, wide open, never full,
although for centuries, layer on layer,
Cornishman, foreigner are laid here.
     Cormorant country, curlew country . . .

Patterns of lines assail me: the vertical
as the line of life: masts, trees, I
still vertical, perpendicular. Boats lie
like bodies of the dead: horizontal:
correct posture for sailing off to eternal
     time country, God country . . .

# THE SPARROW

A little diplomatic sparrow
Very narrow in the hips
Pecked at my window in the dusk.
His beak — a tusk,
Efficiency in his black finger-tips
As dark as coal, as hard as wire.
In his eyes — a frozen fire.

He is a Machiavellian creature.
Adorned in his retiring grey,
Eyes without depth and poignant features,
A quiet domineering way.
He is a democratic bird.
He joins in play the Great Unwashed,
In thick or thin he can't be squashed
And the great war, the next, the third,
Will leave unmoved his round bird's eye.
He never has idealised
The things of life. He asks no why.
But he is safe, industrialised,
There is no mystery for him,
He has known all and realised
That he must sink or swim.

# THE MOON ROLLS OUT

The moon rolls out, hangs at the top of the sky
each darker rib exposed. It is full, it takes over,
pours into creeks, rides on the back of waves,
marks out creased waterways for its load of light.
The boats are firmly glued to its drowned gold face.
The land feels the weight of the moon, attempts to adapt
its late hour breathing to the slow moon music.
Pebbles shift on the beach, the plants are screwed up,
they bend their stems, they stretch. A tree reaches out
for compost round its roots. A fish leaps out,
a seal swims out to the fish. On silent paws
a fox wades out into the water, stares, appears to wait:
the wild uplifted face, the fur of the cheeks
shine savage in the moon. He inhales the night,
the stark and scornful smells of seaweed and fish.

# THE HERON

The river dim with fish is like a harp
And he, bird-minstrel plucking at the stream
Where string of water meets the string of sand
Stoops like a question-mark drawn with a Gothic hand
Stirred by a piece of driftwood and a gleam.
Across the cheekbones, grey, ascetic, sharp
Flits feather-vague a prudence and awareness;
And in the figure now drawn-out and huddled,
Now soft and sloping and now gaunt with squareness,
Reserved, mad, secret and secretly muddled
This longing for a stir, a splash, a trout . . .

# BIRD'S PRAYER

Tree full of leaves, tree of my nest
Watch over me, shelter my rest.

My lord most green, refuge of wings
Protect this bird who builds and sings,

And hatches the appointed brood.
Allow your tenant bed and food.

Grant speed in flight and skill in chase,
Protect your bird, Tree full of grace.

# CANTATA FOR APPLE-VOICES

*Where is wisdom to be found? Under
an apple-tree, by pure meditation, on a
Friday evening, in the season of apples . . .*

*Chorus* (troubled voices)
We do not feel safe,
We do not feel secure.
Green and naked as we are in draughty branches,
Isolated in the stupefying wind,
Perpendicular. Vertical. Lost.
Tossed and retossed in the slice of space.
Bruised by sharp elbows.
Slapped upon the face
In this great stress of weather.
*Reasonable Voice*
We have had intermittent sun, it is true,
In the bright interval we applauded the thrush.
*Chorus* (tired voices)
But emanations of an endless rain
Closed us, hedonist apples in a humid blind,
Ah, drenched us through and through,
Wrecked, racked us to the bursting of the rind.
We are emasculated and depleted,
We have split our identity. We know
This excess of the wind, alas, is not completed.
Us it destroys, as we awake and sleep
And dangle strangely like the weathercock
Or something loosely screwed.
From this well-drained, fertilised compost-heap,
From these imported droppings of manure
We plan safe banquets,
And although in demand in every street
We feel intrinsically insecure
Upon this stress of weather.

*Voices*
Sister-apple, sister-apple,
That vast commotion in the trees:
     Only the thrush, only the thrush
     Braving the weather, rushing, rushed,
     Only the thrush!
Sister-apple, sister-apple,
The squirming in the patch of green:
     Only the worm, only the worm
     In the cubicles of the bean,
     Only the worm!
Sister-apple, sister-apple,
That creaking lumber . . . Can you hear?
     Only fear, only fear
     Phantom-faced among cucumbers,
     Only fear . . .
*Chorus and Single Voices*
O no no no no no this cannot be.
No phantoms and no fear in our fenced garden:
None, but the supplication of the plant
— stretch folded hands —
No fear, but the perennial farewells
Of seasons rattled out on the wheelbarrow
To smoky holocausts in hollow places,
Behind the fastened gate, behind the fences.
We dangle, inattentive congregation,
We rise to hear the gospel of the spring,
We drone to droning summer rituals,
Heavy with dew we kneel, heavy with pleading,
Deeper we kneel at sudden sights of bleeding:
     O strawberry, temptation of the thrush!
     O crimson rose, delirium of the bee!
     O crimson, red and rose, O tragic colour!
Essentially, essentially no dolour,
But only shade, shade only, shade and tone
That only partly splashes, gashes us
And only partly. Does not penetrate

33

Into our pulp and pomace of phosphate,
Superphosphate, nitrogen and potash,
Steamed bone, crushed hoof and horn, lime, basic ash,
Decoction of the drenching nicotine,
Tobacco wash,
Grease-bands and rubber-bands lavender-green
Against the whimsical, the wingless winter-moth
In our fenced garden . . .
*Sad Voice*
I am alone here. Sad here. Tied here. Restless too.
Swing closer. Higher. Swing. For sun's sweet sake.
O soon now. Closer. Swing. Can you not swing?
In this high wind shall I confide to you
My private uncommunicable ache,
My secret uncommunicated sting:
The stirring of immortal intuition
About the Tree, the Human and the Snake.
October paradise was like the wall
Where peaches ripen, clinging and so warm
And some still call this time of year the Fall,
But they do not mean this, not this at all.
*Dreaming Voice*
The past is full of voices. It deludes
With green suggestion. Could I ever be
The fullness filling the palm of the shepherd
Faced by the goddesses? Consider, three!
When us the thought of one lone god bewilders!
*Chorus* (of Cooking Apples)
Forego, forego those pippin-platitudes!
Our fertilisers are best apple-builders
In our fenced garden.
*Troubled Voices*
I have a little sister
She has no pips,
O pluck that little sister
With her thin pinched hips,
O pluck that little sister

In her tight green cassock
She is sick to death of orchards
And her well-cut hassock.
She sizzles and she sizzles
In the moonlit air
And when it drizzles
She washes her hair.
And I hear her weep
Between dangle and dangle:
*Crazy Apple-Voice*
Why must I behold the orchard
from this angle?
Terrible entanglements
I cannot disentangle.
*Troubled Voice*
I hear her toil
Between sleep and sleep:
*Crazy Apple-Voice*
O no soil to clutch
In this compost-heap!
No gods in this place
With burning russet-locks,
No wild-beast tail striking
Across wild-beast buttocks.
O this grafting of corruption
For commercial feasts
Turneth me to pomegranate
On the robe of the high priest,
Turneth me to horned apple,
The flatterer of princes,
Or diminutive and shattered,
The shabbiest of quinces.
O, this munching in the air,
O this sound of grazing herds.
*Reasoning Voice*
Sister-apple, sister-apple
Only birds . . .

*Troubled Voice*
Small birds are sweet, small hopping birds are sweet,
The sight of hopping birds across the leaves.
Nevertheless I fear the sudden manner
In which they cross my path, so crazy and dishevelled
Focussing us with blunt myopic eyeballs,
What danger bringing from behind the gate?
*Chorus* (hypocritical and servile voices)
Into this well-drained kingdom of phosphate
Superphosphate, nitrogen and potash .
This fertilised, this fecund kingdom where
Only sun, wind and rain are raw and bare,
Only sun, wind and rain are rough and loose
And must be seized, trapped, captured, haltered, noosed,
Tied, pulverised, condensed, made straight and smooth,
Bottled, preserved, sprayed at us from syringes,
Installed to rise and set on metal hinges
In our fenced garden . . .
Meanwhile for us this dangling. No eloping.
Meanwhile for us this dangling in the draught.
Meanwhile for us the waiting and the hoping
For hand-and-basket time, the time of plucking.
Think: graded, weighed, picked gently one by one.
Think: straw and sawdust, wool and cardboard nests.
Think: tissue decorations on our chests,
Our shape and shine, our broad circumference,
Our firm and fleshy sides, our gorgeous tops
In our agnostic acquiescent gowns . . .
Laugh we shall, glorified in the fruit-shops
For fifty, sixty-nine, seventy pence . . .

# The Accident

# I HAVE TAKEN VOWS SAYS THE MOON

### I

I have taken vows, says the moon
I am chaste, I am chaste,
but not the winds of the world
and not the waters,
the winds and waters of fertility.
It is astonishing to be in love.
The man and woman embrace,
the child is conceived.
They lie, they stretch, they listen. They hear no sound
of the quite silently approaching soul.
The ancestors look on, the genes converge,
the white beatitudes are heard to sing.
The land that is nowhere is the true home.

### II

I am pregnant.
May the child be healthy.
This is my only wish.

A normal replica of the race
This is my hope.
I dream of destinies to be
watching my shape

imagining an abstract power
chisel with cosmic tools
geniuses and nonentities
saints poets criminals fools

while secret regiments of genes
take over to instal
their faultless programmes into the
unsuspecting cell.

A million combinations lie
powerful in the field
of distinct possibilities;
you can but wait my child.

And if I lived on blackberries
and mushrooms of the field
or dry peyote, would this affect
the future of my child?

And if I prayed continually
would saints, would angels, would
the powers of heaven pin down my child
upon the breast of God?

And is the soul and is the face
and is the pair of eyes
fashioned before the Tree of Life
was sown in paradise?

### III

Little gene, little gene
Where have you been?
Visiting the atom
Who is my queen.

Little gene, little gene
What did you there?
Gathered acres of protein
Under her chair.

Little gene, little gene
What did you next?
Sorted nucleotides,
Got them fixed,

having then hooked electrons
to the eyes,

I attended
molecular interviews.

Who instructs you, little gene,
In your task?
My programme could not be clearer
I do not ask.


## IV

It all goes back to mothers fertile and festive
great with child mothers preening sheltering feathers
preparing for birth joy pain and sacrifice

It all goes back to mothers pregnant and pensive
the warm womb waters and the nine month mooring
breeding — son — daughter — son — inherit the earth

mothers are fumey kitchens larders and cellars
mothers are fields of corn mothers are meadows
mothers are terrible rivers spawning life and death

never forgetting the fathers in their kingdoms of seed
their effortless lightning involvement in the act of begetting
Dad — Abba — papa — father — tata — winner of bread

It is not good for man to be alone. Together we build
your nest, our stranger-child, in holyghost branches
furnished with heaters and love money and moss
the books are here already with hints how to live
both East and West will croon at the foot of your cradle.
This is a thrilling age. Perhaps you will let me
root out the loveliest bits — underneath it is lovely —
O you will treasure life; I shall teach you to crawl
walk — run — swim — sail — fly — drive —
stroke the fur of the world . . .

V

Dormant in your mother's womb
You do not expect
to reserve yourself a room
in your next world

Uncurling in dark abeyance
you hold no thought
how to drape nakedness
in its first coat

Elemental waters rise
to force you out
and backwards sideways on all fours
with a shout

hurled from one ocean to another
like a creature drowning
you are washed out upon the shores:
a newborn being.

Dormant in your mother's womb
you do not foresee
waiting at doors of cottonwool world
a whole committee

of busy cuddling breasts brains eyes
working out your ration
of milk and possibilities:
destinations

Ears tongues lips and flocks of words
roosting round your name
excited eager to impart
the dialect of the Tribe.

And once you're strong enough to lift
the entire baggage
of vowels and of consonants
you will read the message.

## VI

This is the seventh month. I wait, I detect
your curious push and pull, mysterious minnow.
You signal to me in the undercurrent,
small hooded creature swimming towards birth.
I am your lair, your cell, your fortress with walls;
in it you are stuck, you are hoarded, hooked to somewhere,
you grope for nourishment. It swims towards you
bullocks and lambs and fish enter your being
a cornfield knocks at the brain with whispers of land
vineyards orange groves pastures fins feelers hooves . . .
they buffet you, their prey. You are tidal. You are cosmic.

## VII

Outside the walls life rages. The sun lives there.
The moon, a thin sharp tongue tries to suck me out.
A trap-door gapes in the dark — that way lies peril —
gamble — upheaval — birth — danger de mort —
O do not snatch me out of my tadpole dream!

## VIII

Full fathom five my baby swims. O the mind boggles!
Think, I was but a girl approaching a cradle.
Now, this is birth, this pain, this flood, this upheaval
Around me move white gynaecologists
Where would I be without them? Their stiff overalls!
I am a heaving mountain, an alarmed volcano
could someone stop this earthquake between my thighs?
O go ahead, be born, let us get it over
For nine full months I've stewed this human broth
Will furies lap it up? Angels protect it?
I push — I ache — I break — I burst like a shell —
good morning tiny son, welcome to earth,
I'll give you the name of George
because life is a dragon.

## IX

My son is laid before me. His eyes are open.
We look at one another — he knows how to look.
He tries to blow — he gurgles — he is perfect — he seems
  normal —
Why did I fear to have a mongol child?
He sees me upside down, it must be strange.
The ceiling fills him with whiteness. I show him the sky;
he blinks, screws the eyes, looks astonished, space without limit,
he has not met me really, he has no attachments,
he seems so otherworldly in his baby linens
a chaste remote little monk, little anchorite,
the face is round and smooth, a black mane of hair
each one recorded by God . . . his eyes question me
they have the honest gaze of a baby hound
the tiny feet are broad, the hands are dumplings
the toes uncurl, infinitesimal.
I gently tickle one, it is warm as a grape.
I am filled with wonder, amazement.
Who is this child?
He's floated in from nowhere
Did I really make him?
He did not ask to live. I have thrust it upon him,
poor little nakedness,
poor reckless warrior
he has come all this way to pick his death.
Image of God? Perhaps a messenger
whose gurgles camouflage a secret code
Will he be able to speak before he forgets?


## X

Think, I have made a death — a life and a death —
a life for death to eat. A life is a light
I have switched on a light for death to switch off,
but now the light's a baby full of dimples and future.
I am to feed my son — my son is hungry.

44

## XI

I am an ocean of milk, a great fat dairy
the grazing mammal mooing to her young
I have not eaten grass but my milk is good,
my breasts are heavy and huge they wait important,
this is their day their mission they were made for that,
they are impatient untamed I cannot control them,
blown-up like half-balloons, orthodox cupolas
I feel the milk ascend them like a chant.
The child is laid against me: will he know? will he swallow
the untranslatable liquid from the earth's dark bowels?
Immediately he sucks with the soft round mouth,
with the strong sucking toothless gums he plucks
warm milk and wind the little gulps of life,
white milky taste. The pinky tongue licks round,
now he is bound to live — eating is important
even Niobe 'of the golden hair thought of eating'.
I hear the milk pour down along the throat
hiccupy muffled sound a half-drowned gurgle —
He swallows milk with the wind the eater of wind!
He gulps, the wind escapes. I am proud of my son,
his little armpits are ticklish, I call him names:
my flapping baby rook my innocent.
I am his nest, his desert's water-hole
loving and full of teeth: a lioness
here to defend her cub. And now he weeps;
the angels also wept because they saw
that they were made of mud. My son falls asleep.
Purity waits in the room white as a nurse.

# BABYBIRDS, KITTENS

Babybirds kittens
puppies are defenceless
also the human child
I could leave him in
a wicker basket and go,
the baby Moses
or a telephone booth perhaps
then ring the police.
He would lie there unable
to dial the world
picked up in due course no doubt
adopted schooled
somebody would
force ways of life on him
in which he might
not own, not learn to drive
the killer car.

# MY WISHES FOR HIM

What are the wishes that I would
wind about your head?
Beauty? Glory? Wealth? Good luck?
My first wish: faith in God,

unclouded firm to help you climb
an ascending path
hand in hand with your true love;
my last wish

A whiff of wildness, a whiff of joy
so that when all is told
you and your love on the path that climbs
dance at the top of the world.

# A TONIC BOMB SAYS THE CHILD

We crossed the peaceful railway line
trees on either side
"Easy to blow it up just here,"
says the child — and I
responding to his violent thought
"Where conceal the fuse?
How escape? where escape?
our footsteps would mark the grass!"

Going on we trip on wire
rabbit-snares laid
in undergrowth talking talking
bombs — guns — grenades —
"A-tonic-bomb" — says the child —
till horizons fill
with dandelion parachutes
dropping down to kill.

# THOUGHTS ON EDUCATION

Your child has a difficult face — his smile is crooked
my child is gentle straightforward my child is gifted
he listens repeats remembers; the inquisitive why
has settled on the tip of his tongue. I am getting guidance
my brain — (three pounds in weight four inches deep!)
has been alerted attends to its job of dispensing
two thousand millenia of fact condensed and instant.
It's been a whirlwind journey with nomad apes
through water seeking its level desert and cave
a pitiless stormy vastness now and then lit up
by the emerging tool and masterpiece . . .

I tell my growing son: we are born into
the Western world which is becoming cosmic
it seems this cosmic status is ordained . . .
My drawer's full of notes, I shall have to file them
they take or do not take like inoculation.
My ancestors look down from their dead places
they cannot force my hand, they watch my son
the last born — the youngest — the heir
at the bottom of the ladder
they haven't a clue to his fate
they would like him to answer
the questions that got them foxed
the air is throbbing
with their passionate muddled exhortations
the voices swim in:

"Elementary — basic — simple — the Ten Commandments
the act of faith which is dark which is dark as the night
Credo in unum Deum Patrem omnipotentem
do not try to reshape the world it is good enough
think well of yourself and you win — hang on to your goods —
love yourself — on est bien dans sa peau — it's a matter of
    freedom —

49

les chretiens sont les bien heureux les paiens ont tort
have you framed the idea of goodness?
Done anything decent? Realised that God is your father?
Searched for keys of the kingdom?
Close the eyes you will see the Invisible!''
The voices take off. There is a lot that makes sense
and that is not money.
I've read so many books, my head's not clear
not everybody's hit on the road to Damascus.

# MOTHER, MOTHER, WHICH IS BETTER?

Tell me mother tell me why
you have given birth
to a child who's wild and restless
till he goes to earth?
Here to wrestle out of chaos
where all secrets grow
his own secret
bad good neutral?
Does not even know.

Listen mother, let me ask
which do you think is better
wise and prudent as the owl
or mad as the hatter
and but little time for either
to complete the task
who will reap and who will scatter
mother, mother, which is better?

# PREMONITION

Wind over Wales
November
rain — storm —
the mountains darken
bracken darker than amber
gold under bracken

rain over Wales
November
wild water
cruel earth
gorse flower paler than amber
silver under gorse

mist over Wales
November
the ghosts of sheep
ghost-weather
heather sodden and sombre
famine under heather.

# CAR SPLIT IN THREE AS IT HIT LORRY

. . . the way this car broke into three sections
tells its own story . . .

It seems to have gone out of control
snaked down the road and smashed up on
the front of the lorry.

The jury returned a unanimous verdict
of death by 'Misadventure'.

# THE WILD NIGHT HORSES KILL

*The horses killed the driver because he was perfect.*
S. Weil. *Notebooks*

Are death-traps set to catch
and reap the innocent
and gather ripeness in?

The wild night-horses kill
the driver who was good
the sacred is expelled

now you are God's knight-errant
housed in the atmosphere
transparent in the wind

child of the universe
energy soundless voice
my thought lends you a face

O what a baffled look
you must have had when life
was jerked out of the skin

I shall not ever know
and neither can I guess
what was your last thought, child.

My love lends you a tool
to haul me in, a shoal.
I miss you that is all.

# SILENCE

*Le silence de ces espaces infinis m'effraie.*
Pascal

When time had come for me to know this Silence
I realised the Thing was batty; mad;
Dragging chaotic pallors, without violence
Whitenesses flapping. Vast. O, vast is sad.
I begged it: "Rustle like a silk sarong,
Be the cicada, be the cricket: Sing,
Or let me strike you like a silver gong,
Aware that not an inch of you will ring . . . "
I pleaded, pleaded, pleaded: "Why so mute?
I'd rouse you with a chattering of swallows
For I do fear you smuggle the Absolute
Up those great sleeves, those endless loops and hollows
Where stillnesses forever drift and dance."

I shriek at it with my high voice:
It vanishes with muffled elegance;
Icy reserve; apocalyptic poise.

# HAVE YOU ENCOUNTERED ANYONE WHO KNOWS?

A dying man is like a battered tanker
by acquiescent tugs brought into port
then up the estuary to be anchored.
No longer on the market that spare part
which could keep the engines running. Out of stock
the screws the rivets and the ventilators.
Settle among the drowsing algae, wreck,
to be unpicked by hermit crabs and water.
Yet why the protestation, the lament?
Have you encountered anyone who knows
that shapes are darker where your loved one went
into deep water purples greens and blues?
The dead are our explorers. Waste of breath
to raise an angry fist against our death.

# REMEMBERING

Mothers — composers — bees —
creators strong and weak
help me — assist me in
this hard essential task
for it is not two months
since a life was undone
compelling me to this
remembering of my son
his height of stature his
brown shagginess of hair
the gentle golden look
a kind of lion-flower
the gladness that would light
the beauty of his face
the screwed-up sleepy eyes
secreting happiness
a special gift to love
the grace of inner fire
with the attendant warmth
joy music in the air
and often one would glimpse
like shimmering shadow-fish
a dream that would swim up
into the eyes then vanish
the vision of the dream
that was his restlessness
the rivers of desire
the fish he caught was death
burn candle candle burn
the wax of memory
inspire the task in hand
the task is poetry.

# IF YOU WISH TO BE IMMORTAL

If you wish to be immortal
climb into a poet's heart
and the poet, shaking, straining
every muscle of his art
enters into self-forgetting,
steps into the worker-bee
whom the Spirit of the Hive
orders out into the world
to draw out invisible
honey from the universe.

Sun, light breezes, fields of flowers,
bunches, clusters, clumps of colour,
ritual dancing in the hive,
distant pastures beckoning,
pollen, nectar picked and packed
into pollen-baskets held
by stiff hairs to legs attached,
flight and wing-destroying work,
pure and clean metamorphosed
golden liquid drop by drop
secreted in cells of wax.

So a love and so a life
like a many-petalled bloom
in the fields of memory
for nectar and pollen searched.

Grave the absence death decrees.
Emptiness, but for the deep
trail of love and sympathy.
These, the poet, like the bee
grazes on instinctively
in an effort to prolong,

clarify, perpetuate
absolutely vanished life.
There is nothing else but seek
far into the fitful face
of the sun, empty places
of the sky, singing winds,
crying beasts, past the door
where creatures meet.

Deep deep, poet, dip
past the pistils, down the dark
tender-throated nectary
drawing continuity,
so that not a scent be lost,
not a pollen of that life,
every loving thought that bloomed,
beauty courage innocence,
courtesy and elegance,
the sadness of owlish days,
baffled lost perplexity,
wisdom of the thoughtful child,
clear, abiding, every drop
of the nectar brought and saved
in the hearthouse of the hive;
for mysterious honey is
but translated joy and grief.
I know of no other way
of drawing love out of time.

# THE ROOM

Friday's a day for dying. You too died on Friday
I had to let you go, could not possibly stop you.
The room is left behind with trees looking on,
serious and gay with posters, warm in the lamplight.
And now I sort your belongings; they lie about me
spread on the floor, the trophies of twenty-two years.
I divide it all into bundles, here are the papers:
letters, diaries, postcards, photographs, prizes,
recipes how to live, the beautiful mottoes.
Here is the new job contract beginning on
the day on which you were buried, the exciting menus . . .
and here your other skins: dare-devil, knight-errant,
crimson Moroccan stone exchanged for a shirt,
the immense shoes! My poor huge darling child;
I must salute this sock, converse with this button,
over the yellow slipper I weep for a moment,
the old brown sandals talk of Salamanca,
the little red rugby cap runs back to half-term,
the woollen scarf waits at the railway platform
with ruffled schoolboy hearts rebuking the hour.
And now's the day for sunshine pebbles and paddling;
the sea leaks out of the bucket, we picnic under
outlasting tellurian trees arranging the future
memories come and go now absorbed now singing,
outside the jackdaws blacken the chestnut branches . . .
There is an emptiness: my son is elsewhere;
There is a dull defeat: I have no son now;
There is a baffled feeling: my son's everywhere
somehow involved with the world . . . I pack I pack
condensing the decades inside a case.
The case bulges with love. I cannot close it.

# THE EVER MYSTERIOUS VICTIM

Earth is my cradle and home
life upon earth is a gift
nothing more beautiful than
meeting the sun and the moon
animals people and stars
who could outmarvel the wind
the way it sings to a tree
or hills which hold in their hands
the cooling cup of the sea
Life is a marvellous gift
of strictly rationed decades.

The other side of the coin
must be the price each one pays
for the permission to live
the single journey across
incomprehensible earth

A human being can be
as good and exquisite as
the work of art he can make

A being gentle and meek
enough to inherit the earth
walks into shapes that are doomed
Each time there's a shrinking
a shriek
in the pulsing heart of the world

And what is curious and strange
is that often too often the
thoughtless cruel and cold
lead to the cross the ever
mysterious victim.

# NATASHA SAYS

Natasha* says
George is with God
he is not dead

you are a baby if you cry
for George is well.

He watches me
he does not sleep
he can have all

he wants he laughs
the sweets do not
decay his teeth

he listens to me
but does not
answer because

he only smiles
he is a window in the sky

between the stars
when you are naughty
God has to

beat your behind
or else He may
send you to earth

God visits us
when we are good
eats in the kitchen.

*Natasha — aged four.

# LITTLE THOUGHTS

## I

Perpetually I mourn you, tragic boy
too early flown from this rook-rounded house,
friend of the underdog, gay gentle one
wanderer, knight-errant, dreaming Icarus.

I pick the fragments and I hear them bleeding
into the tabernacle of my hurt.
You were the book I had not finished reading
the chapter I have failed to learn by heart.

## II

Move on, great Person to
the other side of the Gate
where Fate hovers not over you,
but you over Fate.

*Translated from the Polish of Norwid*

## III

Picking flowers for your grave
I hear your voice:
"What a crazy thing to do!
I'm with you in the house!
So why must you banish me
to crosses and stones
as if I was only there
guarding skin and bones!"

# A PRAYER

Mother of God with the sharp crescent underfoot,
(I like to see it almost round fumbling through the branches;
I like to see it tangled up in fruit)
    Pray for us now and at the hour of our death.

Mother of God (with the clouds round her stiff as starch,
her veil blue-white, unstarched, a flowing thing)
On all Good Fridays and all Ides of March,
    Pray — awful days do not only come in spring.

Mother of God, little girl playing in the world,
playing with the rose-plant and the time, the time of pruning;
playing with the sun in the hollow places of the wall.
    Pray for us now when you hear us calling and when
            we do not call.

Mother of God beside the Tomb fearfully weeping,
weeping at the back of the hill, in the cleft of the rock,
because we have reason to fear this lying down and sleeping
    Pray for us now and at the hour of our death.

# WHAT ARE THESE BIRDS FOR?

From this high winter field I watch a boat's
Evening return from sea in a cloud of gulls
Announcing fish on board. I am too far
To hear the chugging engine, the screeching sea-birds,
Too far to see the small detail, yet know
That the light, moving, elongated halo
At the stern of the boat are gulls attending
The Ceremonial of the Passing Fish —
The mackerel mound on deck, now mostly dead,
Since it is only swimming makes fish live.
Strange silver life. Lovely mysterious fish
Cool, remote, agile, scaly, beautiful
Now in their bitter fight against extinction:
The staring eyes, the panting agonised gills,
Tail-fins beating the air, the slithering horror —
And how efficiently the fisherman
Tears open silver belly after belly
With the small gutting-knife strips off the flesh
And throws the pale pink entrails to the air;
How inexorably, how softly, quickly
And silently they die — their salt wet life —
The gulls' glad hunger and the setting sun's
Part in this shimmer of eternal endings . . .
This on my left. On my right — unexpected —
By an uncanny kind of symmetry
A bright red plough appears and like the boat
Cuts into the skin of the field unstitching the secret
Dark warm cockroachy life hatched out in the earth,
Insects I do not know cut up in half,
Their wriggly hold on life, beautiful, gruesome.
And once again the loud assembly of birds,
And are they here for Life or Death or Hunger?
Their everlasting screech and squawk, their violent
Milling about, wild beaks scraping the soil —

White splashes brighter than black — what a riddle the world!
And now it is my turn. The Plough of Death
Runs cutting across life its straight brown furrow,
So fat and glistening, undoing the green,
And the birds are here already, the black and white,
Wheeling about the head, mingling their feathers,
Always the mingled feathers, white and black,
The white sea-birds of love, black rooks of grief,
The mingling feathers, the ancestral voices.

# Love Poems and Other Poems

# GREECE IN HAIKUS

Gods of compression
Assist me to describe
My twenty-two Greek days.

Greece of the islands
Confetti thrown by the gods
Into wine-dark sea.

Ossios Laucas:
I buy five yellow candles
From a shaggy monk.

Wild strawberries
Full of warmth sugar and redness
Unpicked on the hill.

Among the icon-lamps
Grieving and grave the dark gold
Byzantine face.

Mule carrying hay
Donkey carrying logs. Mule
carrying woman.

Across the broken arch
And the wild valerian
The vanishing stair.

Very green lizard
Orange beneath the throat — dives
deep into clover.

Broom — orange blossom —
What other anonymous scents
On the light wind?

A woman of stone
meditating upon the
Passing of time.

Delphi — sun — silence —
The touch of ancient fingers
Upon broken stone.

A bee hums in the ruins
I pick from a broken tomb
The tooth of a wild beast.

I touch the column
It leaves a dryish pollen
White on the finger.

Upon these burning stones
Trailed Clytaemnestra's rich
Embroidered robes.

Consoling the hand
Of the goddess — consoling
Across the white brow.

The Python-Slayer
The Vanquisher of Darkness
Calm and pitiless.

The swan — now the bull
What strange alliances do
Godlike creatures make.

In black. Unsmiling
Thin-lipped and burnt by the sun
Old women watch us.

Lady, day is for talk
Night is always for love
And a little sleep.

O let us drink, friend,
To the damnation of
The stiff upper lip.

This playful flicker
Of rudeness on your lips
Must have crazed your lover.

Would you agree that
The human bottom is
A baroque structure?

O do not let us
Be too clever, gentlemen,
Or truth will elude us.

# THE REFUGEE

You came here twenty years ago, a refugee,
You now possess a British passport; qualify
    for the old-age pension.
Your mother is buried in Ireland.
Your husband is buried in Poland, known as
    Russia on recent maps.
Your brother has finally settled in Montreal.
Your sons went to Malaya to fight bandits;
    went to Africa; went to Canada.
Your daughter breeds pigs in Cornwall writing
    verse in a foreign tongue.
Their letters tell you of crocodiles and apes;
    of great elephants perfectly still
Guarding their tusks in wild places;
    of deep winters and huskies and the
Song of the huskies pitched in a minor key.
Of kingfishers and seagulls and the tides of the
    surrounding sea — until you almost forget
The streams of your childhood.

You understand the language of your in-laws. Of yours
    they have now mastered 'tak i nie'.
Your grandchildren (and one is a cripple) do not speak
    your mother-tongue, but they have learnt
    to call you 'Babcia' which means 'grandmother'.
This is one of your happiest words.
Sometimes you are amused to have such a mongrel family.
Sometimes you think 'this is very strange'.
Sometimes you get muddled which language applies to which.
Sometimes you still take to church your native Missal;
    but seldom now — and only by mistake.
You have said that you dream in English.

Until the age of forty you had never
 entertained a divorced person in your house.

Until the age of forty you had not known the word
    'homosexual' — yet you were civilized and
    broadminded and not unduly sheltered.

Until the age of forty you had never been short of money;
    then a friend said 'beggars are not choosers'.
You have never missed church on a Sunday.
You have never been to a psychiatrist
You have never said or thought 'I could not care less'.
You have never allowed your suffering to become a
    mental obsession.
You have considered sin to be the greatest evil.
You are now an old woman of great beauty,
    strong and serene,
At home with the elements, and as it were
    used to taming foreigners, birds and squirrels,
And although — unawares — your face drifts off into
    layers of sadness,
This has only been known to happen when gates
    are closed after children,
Or when — in between courses — a door bangs
    in the draught, and all of a sudden
There is nothing whatsoever to say.

# THE TRAMP

*as soon as they washed him, he died...*

He had not washed for years, well why should he?
King of the open road, tenant of the haystack,
Snoring in barges, dreaming under bridges,
Blowing his nose into wind, scented like a dungheap,
A scarecrow dark with earth, his camouflage?

A femur breaks. Hospitalised and stretched,
Scrubbed disinfected shorn peeled like an onion
Tucked in, pinned down, fed up,
A clean white target;

With swift accuracy death picks him out.

# AN OLD WOMAN

An old woman will wake and uncurl
Her grey petals in front of the fire.
Far from her is the dawn of the world,
Apple-month, month of birth and desire.
     Far from her is the dawn of the world.

Aged-one — and the smell of fresh milk,
As if life meant but udders and cows.
Catkin, catkin on bare winter boughs
Coiling your revelations of silk!
     Catkin, catkin on bare winter boughs.

Would she own that a haunt of magpies
Summoned dreams she would rather forget?
Or that flesh was a house to be let
To a soul and a pair of bright eyes?
     Or that flesh was a house to be let?

And that anguish of dawn and of dusk
Was but weather eroding the part
Of the perishing, perilous husk
Worn by tides both of mind and of heart?
     In the perishing, perilous husk.

Scarecrow, scarecrow admiring the rain
From the coils of your woollen cocoon,
Not for long will your future remain
Round the shallow medicinal spoon,
     Not for long will your future remain.

But beyond blood and blunder and breath
And whatever rejoices or grieves
Come upon the pavilions of death
As a child understanding dead leaves.
     Come upon the pavilions of death.

# HOMO NEANDERTHAL

Sleepless last night because
of heavy wind and gale
I lay imagining
the way I'd fear and feel
in an unpadlocked world
without roof, house, hotel:
world of my ancestor
Homo Neanderthal
on the unsettled floor
of prehistoric cave
reaching for comfort to
his woman and his leaves . . .
How underneath his back
he felt the earthcrust shake
and saw the sacred tree
tremble and splitting crack;
and watched the violent rain
metamorphose into
the terrifying white
of million-winter snow;
adjusting all the time
jigsaw-gods space and time
in the volcanic cells
of the expanding brain.
How — before icecap crept
to swallow broken hill,
before he broke and fell
He found the stillness. Still
for time enough to carve
upon the listening wall,
in clear and loving strokes,
His Bison and his Bull.

# I'D LOVE YOU BETTER

I'd love you better if you loved me well.
I'd hurt you less if you'd communicate
more of your thought and feeling. For how tell
love from indifference or even hate
if not by the expression, by the sign?
The dancer has his dance, the bird his song,
God — the whole universe, his bread, his wine,
but us — with time for ever at our throat
Have thought, thought only and the gift of thought —
All at the mercy of the one poor tongue
and less than half a dozen blundering senses!
O let the dead traffic in silences!
Hound-like upon the scent of your thought, I
Need your good-morning and need your good-bye.

# WATCHED BY A ROBIN

Poet, make sense and frame in words
the intense feeling of the parting moment:
how brown the path underneath the leaves,
how fierce the wind and the sense of loss
and the way they cling to one another —
silent — with time running out . . .
Acorns fall into grass, tears fall on his tie
and into her coat, while close to them a robin
observes them sideways amazed
that human beings can be so motionless — and
are they two or one? — and — that is what counts:
together in a world, watched by a bird.

# TODAY AS ALWAYS

Today as always
this quality of oneness
between us, blend
of tenderness and passion,
stillness and storm
and strong absolving rain . . .

Were we two creatures
mutually bound
within the man-made fence
of law and promise,
would we have kept
this rare divining rod
that leads us to the source
of healing water?

# LANDSCAPE WITH A CURLEW

Reef-rock, oyster-shell, white bone.
Wave rock-broken monotone.
World of hermit-crab and stone.
    Spray in the beat of my wings.

Water rises. Falters. Falls
Loosing seaweed on seawalls.
My mate goes away and calls.
    What love keeps love in a chain?

The seas toss a crested head
In the nest of the seabed.
Life of bird is streaked with red.
    Earth full of cold wind.

The wind turns to go. Returns.
The sun rises, flares and burns.
Follow me across the ferns.
    The parting will eat us up.

Yellow like a field of oats
The moon anchors off and floats
Pouring grief down curlew-throats.
    It is better not to know.

I searched in widening circles. Found
In patches of purple ground
A stone — absolutely round.
    In patches of ground — a stone.

# THE GARMENT

My love, you are the garment that I wear,
The warm, dream-woven tightly-buttoned coat,
The binding spell against the chilling air.

How to protect you against moth, take care
No damp invades, damaging hem or throat?
My love, you are the garment that I wear.

I had once feared that it may tire or tear,
or turn into the worn outmoded coat,
That binding spell against the chilling air,

Having known garments fall beyond repair,
Stored out of sight, for jumble sold and bought;
My love, you are the garment that I wear.

This one — I'll keep: hem altered here and there,
Patched-up the way old sewing-women taught
The binding spell against the chilling air,

Keeping the simplest cut — the simple is rare —
As simple as the sail-cloth for a boat —
My love, you are the garment that I wear,
The binding spell against the chilling air.

# CONCERNING LOVE

*Terminate torment of love unsatisfied — the greater torment of love satisfied.* T.S. Eliot

*What caused him consolation in his sitting posture? The candour, nudity, pose, tranquillity, youth, grace, sex, counsel of a statute erect in the centre of the table, an image of Narcissus purchased by auction. . .* James Joyce

London and the first cherries. Early June.
London, some strike or other. And the heat.
Like apparitions from the *Geographic Magazine*
Women in frocks of puce and tangerine
Preen themselves in the sunny patches of the street
Suggesting ease, voluptuousness and roses:
Feeling partly conveyed, by the street-organ
  and the tune:
Tralalala, your tiny hand is frozen.
Alas, that tiny hands should freeze in June
And such a June, such stillness as if nothing stirred.
Then, suddenly, the crazy interruption of a bird
Switched off abruptly, sound from unacceptable wave-lengths.
The sun slipped like a yellow cat across the pavements,
Dipped into cul-de-sacs. One could not tell
What backyard swallowed it.

  I rang the bell.
(Doors behind which you find, spill, spend and loose
  your passion . . . )
Noting — the way one makes a mental note —
The rigour in the throat
And the mind's dwelling, dallying. The mind
Clutching the safe, the flat;
Fearing the most, most probable collision,
Need of admitting error and declining,
Need of renouncing, making a decision.

Fearing all that
The mind withdraws lollopingly into the heat
Back to the yellow sun, the yellow cat,
Back, back to the street-organ and the street.
(Not that the street or the street-organ care)
But the next moment takes you to his room
Draped in a kind of mahogany gloom
With — in the background — chestnut trees in bloom
And sound of discreet footsteps on the stair.

"So you have come. You have. You came. Your hair —
Long? Short? Your eyes — gold? Green? You change like opal
And have I ever seen you so, in white
And always trailing round that air of peace?
I've been to Turkey, I have been to Greece,
Have you not sensed my thoughts from Constantinople?
O how I wish to God that we could write.
One feels so inarticulate, so lame.
You must have felt me whispering to your ear,
        all the same?"

                Hugging some sad and sensuous idea
                Indeed, indeed I felt that you were near.
                (But that is left unsaid.)

"I search, I search
While not yet altogether cracked and set.
When I see beauty I fall off my perch."
        (poised so intriguingly upon the chair!)
"And now that we have met, now will you dare?"

                "Dramatic question!"

"Pick it up, with caution.
Might not this be our apex of expansion?
Might not this be our summit of emotion?
Consider. Think. It takes a little while
To — well — discard the bag of tricks that's youth
Allowing what the heart has long compiled
Against the awful discipline of truth.

I speak of what I only can presume."
He bears across the mahogany room
The long profile of an Etruscan tomb
In sharpnesses suggestive of a hawk
And when the conversation is resumed:

"I do not even know yet if you smoke,
Do you smoke?
For although I have dragged your life with guesses — "
    (stands he or sits he, does he talk, with whom?)
"I cannot really think of what you do
When you discard your city-suit, your fame,
The little heap of letters behind your name —
Plant hollyhocks in green suburb recesses?"

"Will you believe me if I say I think of you?"

"Yet if I heaped you now with all my yesses
In the consent there would be no elation . . . "

"Then why stray into areas of temptation — "
(what a bizarre description for this room,)
"Unless for revelling in revelations
Desirable on this side of the tomb?"

And why indeed!
At this point, on this level,
At this emotionally drastic curve
We might as well attempt to learn reserve
To make our inner beings less dishevelled.
Besides, do not our passions somewhat lack in heat?
Stretch, stretch your hand and feel that mat of sun
The little nude Narcissus leans upon,
Bringing to mind some cases up our street:
Tristan, Heloise, Cleopatra, even Swann.
But this? It does not matter, does not matter, does not matter
I shall spend my life, a squatter
Among the icicles . . .

The room appears to listen in
On words that rise, on words that fall.
The alabaster figurine
Sips aphrodisiac by the wall,

And liquid alabaster eyes
Shameless and lustrous like veneer
Observe the coupling of the flies
Upon the crystal chandelier,

Blinking in effort to recall
Some green anonymous excess
While in the room words rise and fall
Stirring the yellow silences;

Lovely, Rotten
Love in your little dress of cotton

What a waste
To let you go like this, without a taste

Taste, then, take.
We shall sleep a thousand years, never wake.

Enough, enough
Your mouth is very terrible and soft.

Right or wrong,
O love gambols very glibly on the tongue.

Words that would lead to a caress
Collapse in the substantial dust
Within the circle of the dress
Piling their little loads of lust

Sybilant phrases sift and spin
And swoop more palpable than stone.
The alabaster figurine
Views agonies of flesh and bone

And glows beneath the marble skin,
Inviolate on the marble stem
Scanning the ways of love wherein
Lies such absorbing stratagem.

Love wild. Love bridled — tame and mild:
"It was a pleasure." — "Not at all."

Life is the bright inflated ball
Bounced low by the exhausted child.


When thought is mixed with moonlight — black and blue
Black thought, blue moonlight, the confused — the clear —
I hesitate. A moment only. True,
Here is my life curled up inside the chair
So light and languid, vulnerable through you;
Here is the heat, a part of the nightmare
And there the cold — and chose between the two.
IT IS THE BLEAK IT IS THE BLANK THAT SCARE.
These ambiguities provide no clue.
Blame them on night that rises from the sill
To swamp the mind (a narrow thoroughfare);
On body swayed by rhythms of the pulse.
Blame it upon the face, upon the hair!
What is the use of beauty since it will
Draw what must be refuted and repulsed?
O bright eternal calmness of the air,
These old catastrophes must hurt us still.
IT IS THE BLEAK, IT IS THE BLANK THAT SCARE.

# WHEN I RETURN TO POLAND

When I return to Poland I will find it altered
Moved like a building-block from East to West
Still taming, still adjusting its new map-places.

When I return to Poland after fifty years
Three friends will be there to greet me with gifts of mushrooms
Picked in the Torun forest, and Holy Week palms.
Someone somewhere will say "But you have an accent!"

When I return to Poland I shall be astonished
To hear my native language talked on street corners
Freely — alive and kicking — intelligent — vital — ;
Astonished to see the fields being ploughed by horses,
Well-cared for, gleaming horses returning from market
With — often — a cow in the fura — the long wooden
       carriage.
Chickens will scratch by the roadside unafraid of traffic;
Churches will burst at the seams and ancient buildings
Restored after bombs will bow and plead for attention.

When I return to Poland I shall be invited
to read my long-age poems in a place of learning.
The room will be full of professors. They will listen, attentive.
In the back of the room, amidst them, Mother Tongue wearing
a robe of mystical gold — liturgical — hieratic —
(I see her always in gold, the Mother of Words)
Her pensive face, the gesture of hand absolving
this Prodigal Daughter who squandered, scattered
her heritage of words in foreign lands.

When I return to Poland an unknown poet
Will offer me yellow freesias. In my Square of Emotion
Two giant horses will stand in the moistened air

On patient powerful feet, high priests of that land,
With pale-pink pompoms dancing round their ears;
They will turn their heads towards me, beckoning, laughing
with soft benevolent mouths, curving their lips
in a deep horsy laugh, offering friendship —
The gurgly homecoming laugh . . . I shall stroke and kiss
Their velvet muzzles, their sloping chestnutty cheeks
With darkness around the eyes and weep a little
Smelling the meadows in them, smelling Poland in them.